CW01508123

A Walk with Words

Armorel Allen

First published in Great Britain in 2021

Copyright © Armorel Allen

The moral right of this author has been asserted.

All rights reserved.

Design, typesetting and publishing by UK Book Publishing

www.ukbookpublishing.com

ISBN: 978-1-914195-29-7

Reflections on the Camino de Santiago

The Camino de Santiago is an ancient and well-trodden pilgrimage route in Northern Spain. Upwards of 300.000 pilgrims arrived in Santiago de Compostela in 2019. The pandemic in 2020 reduced the numbers able to travel the Way which was inaccessible to many for a large part of the year. There are many "caminos". This book relates to the 500 miles from St Jean Pied de Port on the French side of the Pyrenees, to Santiago de Compostela in Galicia.

The poems were written along the Way, flowing almost daily as Armorel walked, initially solo, later with fellow pilgrims who soon became dear friends. It is intended that the words will resonate with those who have made their own pilgrimages – not only on the Camino de Santiago, but on the many paths we all walk through life.

The poems are presented in the order in which they were written, with a short description or context – very few place names are recalled, apart from (obviously) the start and finishing points.

Dedicated to all who travel hopefully

In St Jean Pied de Port, people of all ages, from around the world, assemble to start their pilgrimage at the French side of the Pyrenees. Staying for a night or two in the charming little town provides a chance to recover from jet lag, or previous travels and allows people to start to know others. Many travel in pairs, or groups but also solo. As this was my second Camino, there was much interest in why I was repeating it.

CAMINO

Camino calls, it calls to you.
Take the path you know is true.
Each one travels his own way-
Time to think, give thanks and pray.

Camino tests, it makes you ask
Why you've taken on this task.
Helps you look so deep inside:
All those hopes and fears you hide.

Camino gives without a doubt,
Makes you want to weep and shout.
Ask for help and it will show
From someone you have yet to know.

Camino teaches many things;
Also many blessings brings –
Friendship, openness and strength
Manifest along its length.

Camino calls you, calls you back;
The hills, and mountains, dusty track.
So much pain and joy are found
As you walk this hallowed ground.

Camino knows your deepest dreams.
All is never as it seems.
Like our lives, Camino bends,
Ever onward, never ends.

Day One, the path ahead was steep and rose relentlessly before me. All sorts of worries assailed me

Would I injure myself slipping on the uneven ground? Is my backpack too heavy? Will I get blisters? I noticed last time that people who set a fast pace would be encountered later with all sorts of problems– this is for the long haul, and different to a day's hillwalking at home – muscles and joints may protest at being pushed too hard repeatedly.

I was encouraged by fellow travellers as I climbed up and over the Pyrenees. The Camino spirit of camaraderie is evident right from that first awful slog up to Orisson. The spectacular scenery was a welcome distraction too.

A PATH WITH HEART

Pilgrim, take the path with heart,
When it calls you, make a start.
In your backpack place your woes,
Your love, your gratitude, wish to grow.

Every day you leave at dawn,
Light comes slow as day is born.
Many miles you'll walk along
With your thoughts, perhaps a song.

Feet get tired but heart grows strong;
You will know that you belong
On this ancient well-trod way,
With other seekers, day by day.

When at night you come to rest
You will know you've done your best.
Open up your heart to others –
All are pilgrim sisters, brothers.

If by chance you take a fall
Others help, each is for all.
Body, mind and heart and soul:
All a part of one great whole.

When walking alone, silently, sometimes my thoughts were pierced by snatches of conversations as others passed me by.

FRAGMENTS

Floating words as you pass them by
"He died..." "don't get it…" "want to cry…."
Flowers in colours pink and blue,
Clouds, mown fields, a stone in shoe.
Stop for coffee, rest the feet
A new Camino friend you'll meet.
Moving on and letting go,
Some swift of pace and some more slow

So many of us are attached to our phones these days, and on the Camino, it is a useful resource for booking accommodation or finding the correct way (if the yellow arrows are not spotted). I tried to resist the lure of technology as much as I could – there was so much else to see/hear/feel.

PROGRESS

Early morning, day is growing.
In the East some light is showing.
Pilgrims walk in nature's ease,
Birdsong gently breaks the peace.

Fields of sunflowers, new mowed hay
Show the ancient farming way.
Now the walker checks his phone;
Some, reflecting, walk alone.

Changed, the way that pilgrims walk.
Some prefer to chat and talk.
Are the times so deeply other
That thoughts and prayers are not discovered?

Each will find out what is needed;
People change, the new is heeded.

*Of course, every day is different. There is a saying that the first
third of the Camino is physical – this is where your body gets used
to the stresses and strains you are placing on it. The final third
is a spiritual challenge, whereas the middle third is where I once
again faced my personal (mental) demons*

THE DARK SIDE

No-one to talk to on the way.
No-one to take the pain away.
Why did I set out on this quest?
Always, I have to know what is best.

Questioning my motives, asking myself
What did I hope to learn about health?
'Get up and walk' I blithely say.
Don't feel much like that today.

Am I a loner? Not part of the crowd?
Can't I accept love? Is that not allowed?
Trying my hardest to keep a brave face,
But needing and wanting a moment of Grace.

Keep walking, keep asking these questions of God.
Who cares if the others just think that I'm odd.
I'll walk with the pain, the sadness, the low,
Even if my mind's burdens are making me slow.

The sun shines, the fields glow and flowers open up.
I'll sit in the fresh air and have one more cup.
Today I am painful, tomorrow who knows?
But surely, please Spirit, your message will show.

People talk about miracles that happen along the Way. After my pity party, the next person I met was a young woman from Korea. Her name is Cecilia, and after this encounter, I never saw her again. Camino magic? St Cecilia is the patron saint of Music! (Music is a big part of my normal life, which I had to leave at home.)

CECILIA

After the storm of tears and fears.
After the plea for a sign,
Cecilia came to me, quite unawares
And helped me to re-align.

She talked of music in foreign places,
Asked me about my life.
Helped to locate the hidden traces
Of grief, which she managed to shift

She sang a sweet song she knew that I'd know -
I couldn't join in for tears.
The tune was the wonderful "Gabriel's Oboe"-
It drove out my worries and fears.

So thank you, Great Spirit for listening to me;
I know that my problems are small.
But you take great care of the least of your flock
And tenderly cherish us all.

It seemed that as the journey progressed, the sights and sounds of nature became ever more important to me, overshadowing any physical discomfort or mental distress. I found I was noticing my surroundings in a different way.

MESSAGES

A little bird brought me to morning today:
It fluttered ahead when too steep got the way,
Then flew in the hedgerow to once again show
When the struggle was hardest, she'd come say hello.

Nature beckoned me on, the hill was quite high.
The trees and the bushes all seemed to say "hi,
You've made it this far, though you've suffered some pain,
Some sunshine. some laughter, some downpours of rain."

And now, as the sun makes its way in the east,
My anguish is quelled, for the moment at least.
I see all the beauty our Maker provides
As we wander through life with our spiritual guides.

Being a parent, my family were never far from my thoughts;
sharing personal stories with other pilgrims reminded us of who
is important

NEAREST AND DEAREST

Today as I wander, I think of my dears:
My son and my daughters, their hopes and their fears.
I remember them little, their faces so sweet,
Their tummies. their bottoms, their perfect wee feet.
How I loved and I love them, these children of mine.
My heart fills with thanks – all we shared for a time.

All grown up and gone on to fulfil their destiny,
But nothing can change how much they still mean to me.
I miss you, I love you, my closest of kin.
May your lives bring you joy and be free of grave sin.
You have so much before you to share and impart,
And you'll always be with me, at least in my heart.

In the stillness, I sometimes found bizarre concepts floating round my mind, though seeming perfectly sensible at the time. I found this metaphor intriguing.

BIRTHING

At conception, the Camino pierces the ovum of the soul.
When time and motive are right, the
idea grows- the body changes,
Prepares for the ordeal ahead with great anticipation and joy.

At onset the sudden pains and fears as reality kicks in-
Pushing on, with each ascent and descent growing,
The labour pains become more intense.

Fellow pilgrims are the doulas, encouraging, holding,
Sharing each moment. Angels along the way
Give help and tips and bandage toes.

The gripping pain subsides, gives respite
Mental ones replace those woes.
Can you do it? No escaping, only way is through the woes.

Towards the end a mighty climax- this will be the last ascent.
What is birthed? A new adventure-
Camino enters into life.

Other days, all was tranquil: the presence of a Higher Power almost palpable.

PEACE

In God is the stillness, in stillness is God.
We are taking the pathway which millions have trod.
In the distance church bells so tunefully ring:
In the present heart wakens, commences to sing.
All quiet, save birdsong and steps on the trail.
We wander inside ourselves in search of the Grail

One of my favourite experiences on the Camino was getting to know people from all around the world. Sharing stories, truly hearing the other – there is an abundance of authenticity:

PILGRIMS

People want to stop and talk,
Rest the feet before the walk.
Where're you from? Where did you start?
Then, outpourings from the heart.

Some are missing those at home.
Some are always on the phone.
Some have come to heal a loss:
To lay to rest their weighty cross.

All have stories, most will share
Hopes they have and what they fear.
Open-hearted, open minds,
Leaving prejudice behind.

This connection feels so right-
Makes the future look so bright.
Heart to heart our truths we share.
Brotherhood of man is here.

As I adjusted to this simple pace of life, carrying only basic essentials and trusting that the road would unfold, gratitude came to the fore. There is so much in this world that we are privileged to enjoy:

PRAYER

Moon glows, a silvery light ahead
As sunrise paints the fields gold red.
The vista stretches far and wide.
Nothing disturbs the calm, inside.

How beautiful to walk this earth,
To know that every step is worth
A thousand prayers of gratitude
And praise for God's beatitude.

All sorts of people set out on this pilgrimage, each with their own motive – whether religious, spiritual or for sport. Many do not know why they are here – they are simply compelled to do it. Months, sometimes years of preparation may have been undertaken and all become experts on the best equipment, the "right" footwear, the correct way to manage blisters.

DIVERSITY

They gather from all round the globe it seems,
When they feel the Camino pull.
All clothed by Decathlon and REI
And a lot of merino wool.

Some fall in love as they journey along:
Their bliss is a joy to behold.
For others, deep friendships are found and shared,
With as much love as heart can hold.

There are grumbles and gripes as is always the case
And worriers, anxious of all.
Veterans used to alternate life-
Some speedy and some at a crawl.

There are many who think they are here just for sport,
Determined to have a ball.
But Camino spirit is undeterred –
Miracles happen to all.

Leaving the hostel before dawn, walking alone was an incredible experience. The sun rose behind me (as the path goes from East to West,) but there were plenty of chances to turn and watch the beauty of the sunrise.

LIBERATION

I love this time in the morning
When there's no-one about but me.
The sun is still sleeping, the moon and the stars
Give light enough for me to see.

I love this time in the morning-
My stride is determined and long.
And tap, tap, tap go my sticks on the road –
A heartbeat as I walk along.

I love this time in the morning.
My mind is unfettered and free.
Words and ideas fill up my head.
It's a time that is precious to me.

Walking for miles, especially in the Meseta, which is flat farmland with very distant horizons, I thought of all the people in the world. Such a privilege to have the time and health to do this, though there are many pilgrims who come with health problems, both physical and mental. It is a place of healing.

THANKFULNESS

I travel this road with gratitude
For all that my life has given.
My family, friends and acquaintances;
Those moments that felt like heaven.

I travel this road with pain in my feet,
My backpack heavy at times.
I walk and I pray and send up love
And notice when church bells chime.

I travel this road for others
Who cannot consider this trail.
Perhaps they are not ready mentally-
Perhaps they are physically frail.

I travel this road to atone for my past.
I know that I must make amends
And though I am journeying solo
There's always the chance to make friends.

I travel this road for the hopeless:
The lost and forlorn souls,
Who just need a nudge to go into the Light
Where Great Spirit will make them whole.

I travel this road to make friends with myself,
To be glad for the life that I live.
So that when returned home I can hopefully show
That there's still so much more I can give.

I travel this road in solitude:
I travel this road with gratitude:
I travel this road to think and pray:
I travel this road for a better way.

*Of course, leaving in the dark, there were times when I missed the
yellow arrows if my torch was shining in the wrong place!*

GUIDANCE

I took a wrong turn, as is often the case.
I'd travelled along in the dark.
Only noticed when looking around me-
no arrow, no Camino mark.
For quite a long time I had stumbled along- I
thought that the way would come clear,
But something felt strange, I was clearly
amiss- no pilgrims were anywhere near.

I stopped and again I asked for a sign,
and far in the distance could see
Some torchlight, way back, going off to the
West – the way I was meant to be.
I turned back and walked down the lonely dark
road, I followed the way of the Light.
And once again joined the pilgrimage route,
with confidence that it was right.

The daily routine of the pilgrim is a simple one. Walk, shower, eat, chat, sleep......... repeat. The hostels (albergues) are usually pretty basic but meet our needs, though each place has an individual character. Some are run by religious orders, some municipal, some privately owned. Each one is a welcome sight on the road.

REFUGE

Hostels, gathering, resting places;
New arrivals, well-known faces.
Is there a lower bunk to spare?
Should boots and walking poles go there?

Laundry outside. The line is full.
Will our stuff dry? It's very cool.
In the kitchen, sharing our food:
It tastes nutritious, does us good.

Maybe a glass or two of red?
Helps us to sleep when we get to bed.
Early to bed and early to rise.
We're all the same, we realise.

As the days marched on, and I got caught up in my own inner world, it is not surprising that simple things were sometimes overlooked – possessions left at an albergue, at a coffee stop, under a bunk, hanging on the clothesline. This did lighten the load somewhat!

LOST AND FOUND

Broken headlamp, misplaced poles,
Broken spirits, wayward souls.
Something lost along the way
Reappears another day.

Sense of humour, sense of fun,
Sometimes seem to hide from one.
Then again empathic feeling
Oftentimes can leave you reeling.

Into cities, through the towns;
Lost, in circles, round and round.
Stop to work out where you are-
Others help. You'll not stray far.

Day by day the feeling grows,
Something somewhere somehow knows
What you need to guide you home.
Never henceforth quite alone.

Part of the Camino is along an ancient Roman road – straight as a die, for miles and miles. It can be daunting to walk in the heat of the midday sun, no shade, no shelter. A small bend in the road is cause for great rejoicing – and photographs!

TWISTS AND TURNS

Sometimes the road is gently curved
And others oh so straight.
The endless highway stretches on
Your senses start to grate.

A coffee stop, a bathroom too,
You wish with all your might.
You count your steps, you carry on
Till in the distance – lights!

Those parasols, those plastic chairs:
A refuge there you'll take,
Then wander on for many miles
Until another break.

Sometimes the path is difficult,
A challenge for the soul.
But always there's a way to reach
Your Santiago goal.

At times I was overcome with a feeling of bliss, surrendering to the moment I was in:

STILLNESS

Deep is the peace which my soul has come to know.
Strong is my heart as onward I will go.
Calm is my mind; my thoughts are held in check.
Tested is my body as I keep on with my trek.

*This sense of serenity deepened and in the quiet, filled my heart
until it had to find expression:*

EPIPHANY

It's all about love, I've come to see.
First love Great Spirit who then enfolds me.
Love for my brother, my sister, my friend.
Love for the whole world without any end.
Love for the sun which warms up my back,
Love for the pilgrim who carries her pack,
Love for the ones that send on ahead,
And love for the fearful who long for a bed.

Love for the mountains, the rivers, the plains,
Love for the sunshine, the mist and the rain,
Love for the insects that pepper the ground.
Love for the birdsong, that beautiful sound.

Love for the weary, the hurting, the sore.
Love for the hearty – the ones who want more.
Love for the quiet, reflective souls,
Who focus their minds and consider their goals.

Love for the dear ones who seem far away,
Love for the travellers I meet on the way,
Love for the world and everyone here,
Love for each other, it all becomes clear.

One of the high points (literally and figuratively) is the Cruz de Ferro – the Iron Cross, at the top of a hill. Pilgrims bring a stone from home and add it to the enormous pile placed there by others over the years. I stopped for a while, a chance to reflect, and to symbolically leave behind my troubles.

CRUZ DE FERRO

We lay our stones at the Iron Cross
and with them place a prayer
For all the souls who travelled long and far, till they are here.

It's said our burdens will be shed if placed within a rock.
We reverently stand awhile and of our lives take stock.

We carry stones for those we love, their burdens too we share.
We send out love for all to have. We think about our cares.

The Iron Cross stands tall and proud-
the high point on the hill.
So, lightened now of all our woes, we wander onwards still.

Day after day, I continued walking, deepening the connection with nature and taking me ever more into my inner realm. The outside world seemed far away and the only reality was the moment I was in:

MEDITATION

Yesterday, the sky blushed deeply
As the sun rose and took command of the day.
Today, a misty stillness
Cools us as we set upon our way.

No sound, 'cept birds
Accompany our walk.
It's time for inner solitude.
Not now a need for talk.

Each day the same yet different;
The footsteps carry on,
But mind and spirit grow and swell-
Such thoughts to dwell upon.

The mists will clear, the sun will shine.
We'll soon be hot and tired.
So now enjoy the quiet
And the chance to be inspired.

To walk for miles, with a pack on my back, for days and weeks on end, took its toll on my body. There was no way to avoid the unaccustomed strain and minor damage – the only thing to do was to keep walking.

RELEASE

Old injuries flare up, awaiting a healing –
That bad knee, that sore toe, that neuralgic feeling.
You keep plodding on, ignoring the ache
In the hope that time is all it will take.

But something is needed to help it resolve-
A bandage, a plaster, a pill to dissolve.
Old wounds will show in the strangest of ways-
Thoughts of a break-up, the loneliest days.

No way to repair them, those ghosts of the past:
Send love out anyway and hope it will last.

As the pilgrimage continued, I formed bonds with individuals, so that although still solo, I had company when it was needed. In the final weeks, the challenge ahead would be the mountain track leading to the village of O'Cebreiro, in Galicia. It was amazing how the landscape changed, becoming very like Scotland: the same wildflowers grow here.

PERSISTENCE

Hills as far as the eye can see.
We're travelling slow, my companion and me.
At first in the dark we are led by the stars
Then daybreak- the mountain looks not very far.

Up, up, up on stony ground,
River and birds the only sound,
Save for the deep and laboured breathing.
Stop, look back at what we're leaving.

Rest awhile, admire the view.
Only one goal we must pursue.
Get to the top and find a bed-
A place to lay the pack and head.

In Galicia now it seems:
Heather, holly, oaks and green
Green pastures, mist and trees.
The rolling landscape spirit frees.

Then at the summit, a pretty town.
Spectacular views are all around.
Time to enjoy a well-earned break.
Our feet to rest, our thirst to slake.

Ascending the mountain, the weather may be fine, the visibility excellent, but at this elevation, it can be cold at night. The hostels and the village were busy, as bus trips frequently come to this place. The church holds a daily pilgrims' mass, as do most churches in the villages passed through. So, after a blessing, a meal and a good night's sleep, the journey carried on.

RESILIENCE

What a difference one night makes.
Yesterday sun, this morning breaks
With cloud all round, no hills are seen,
'Cept when it clears, a flash of green.

Up and down and round about.
The path is certain, there's no doubt
That down this mountain we will go,
As sure as waters round us flow.

From time to time the mists rise clear:
Green fields and hills do reappear.
The glow of sun will briefly reign,
But soon the clouds descend again.

The heights are waiting, heart grows strong.
Inside you know you'll carry on.
A coffee stop, a cake to share
And 'fore you know it, you are there.

The refuge opens up its door,
Passport, credential, nothing more.
A pittance given for a bed,
A drop of wine, a crust of bread.

And soon renewed you waken to
The morning waiting just for you.
Not long to go, you hope and fear-
Perhaps to come another year?

This route has seen all manner of people walking, from sinners seeking papal indulgences, those paid to walk for their patrons and thereby gain absolution for the sins of the same, to more familiar names like St Francis of Assisi, Charlemagne and more recently Shirley MacLaine, Paulo Coelho, and the stars of the inspiring film "The Way" to mention a few.

MUTUALITY

Many before this path have trod,
Offered up prayers, gave thanks to God.
Under our feet we feel the trace
Of those who earlier came to this place.

Carrying little they travelled far-
Not for those long gone a plane or car,
But trusting God would get them there,
They walked, they talked, they too would share.

So it is now with greater speed
The pilgrims carry what they need,
Lean on each other and share the load
On this, our sacred pilgrim road

There are some spots on the Camino where an alternative route may be taken – to a historic location perhaps, and such is the diversion to Samos, where the oldest functioning monastery in Europe is situated. I took this route and found a vast complex of ancient buildings, manned by only 7 monks nowadays, the oldest being in his 90s. The accommodation offered to pilgrims is basic, and although a mass is said daily, I decided to give it a miss.

SAMOS

Last night I slept in a cold, cold bed
With the ghosts of the past all around.
Pilgrims disturbed my fragile sleep
As they staggered bathroom bound.

Last night the room was damp and dark,
The blankets too were stale.
So many have slept in this ancient place-
My rest was somewhat frail.

Today my mood is quite subdued,
My feet are feeling pain.
But when with sleep I am refreshed
I will set off again.

As the weeks and the miles were consumed and I got nearer to Santiago, a wistfulness developed – in some respects it was wonderful to be nearing the goal, but in others, the end was getting close and I could not imagine re-entering normal life.

GATHERING

Sitting on a mountain top,
Pilgrims passing by,
Still is the morning air:
Sweet the birds do cry.

Trees all around with leaves
Readying to fall,
Laden with sweet chestnuts,
Fruitful, giving all.

Has the load been lifted?
Is the message clear?
Do you know why you were called
To walk and ponder here?

Sweet to have good company-
Helps to laugh and share,
Knowing that you're not alone-
That friendships flourish here.

Many are the pilgrims,
Varied are their goals.
Single is the motive
To help us know our souls.

Each one carries baggage,
Differing in weight,
Helping each the other,
Realise our fate.

Soon will come the winter,
Memories will be gone,
But warmth and love and sharing
Are what we carry on.

Spanish schools sometimes send parties of teenage students to walk part of the Camino and they are understandably chatty and just having a good time with each other. Meeting them at the later stages of my pilgrimage, I found my senses jarred, having become used to peaceful, reflective ambling!

RESPITE

I will walk on through the hip and knee pain,
Through the mists and the crowds and the drizzle and rain.
The downpour continues, my steps keep on going.
I'm soaked to the skin but my spirits are glowing.

How lucky am I to be here in this place,
To ponder and wander and not have to race,
And though a bit vexed with the girls and the boys,
I'm blessed to have hearing, to witness their noise.

So many have joined us to walk on the Way,
It makes quite a difference all through the day.
The new ones don't bother, or maybe don't know
The traditional greeting of "Buen Camino".

And then at the last we arrive at Portos
Drenched to the skin but no longer cross.
The hostel is busy but friendly and small-
Our room is delightful: it was a good call.

Still raining outside as the pilgrims pass by.
Goodbye to one sister: it' s hard not to cry.
But that is the way and a factor of life,
These pockets of friendship, a respite from strife.

I experienced times when the veil between the worlds seemed very thin and it felt like I was surely in the presence of a Higher Power. Such moments of transcendence are truly to be treasured.

INTENTION

Breathe O Great Spirit, breathe into my soul.
Let your presence sanctify and help to make me whole.
Breathe O Great Spirit, lightening the load.
Show the path of love you've taught as
I've walked down this road.
Breathe O Great Spirit, your grace into my heart.
So when at home I then can share the lessons you impart.

Getting close to Santiago, my conflicting feelings grew stronger – excitement- the end is almost here, and dread – the end is almost here. The prospect of resuming a more normal life, without the daily companionship of people I had grown to love and trust deeply was at times overwhelming. But pulling myself back in to the "now" was required, and my senses were sharpened, every instant treasured and noted.

IMMINENCE

We are given the gift of this new day,
For counting our blessings along the Way.
Mists cover the fields in feathery fronds
Till the warmth of the sun lifts the moisture beyond.

Spiderwebs dangle from bushes and hedges.
Gradually landscape appears at the edges.
Shadows precede us, the sun warms our backs:
Happy are we to be treading these tracks.

Not long to go now. Each moment we savour,
Hoping, in real life to carry the flavour
Of life as a pilgrim with love in our hearts
When coming up soon, it is time to depart.

As I approached Santiago, there was a build-up of houses, air traffic (the path goes alongside the airport) and general civilisation. It was quite a jolt to be thrust instantly into the 21st century by a vast and noisy metal bird careering not so very high above me. There was one last coffee stop before the road into the city: a final chance to reflect on the Way.

ACCEPTANCE

Enough, my body is speaking to me,
You've walked a long way, time now just to be.
Be in the moment, a rest you have earned
With time to process all the lessons you've learned.

Enough of the churches we've stopped at to pray.
Enough of the strangers we've met on the way.
It's been a great journey, of that there's no doubt,
With friends, and just solo, now time to get out.

The way is beginning and not at an end.
There's home and there's family to cherish and tend.
Enough is the lesson, though it has been tough,
I've learnt at the finish that I am enough.

·

Printed in Great Britain
by Amazon

60257194R00026